A TIME OF

Stories from Around the World

These stories come from all over the world, and the people in them face all kinds of difficulties and troubles. A woman in Canada and a man in Singapore feel the pain of broken marriages. Young men in Nigeria and in Australia set off on journeys that may not be successful, and will certainly be dangerous. Young couples in India and in Singapore battle against illness and homelessness. In Trinidad an old woman waits for her fisherman husband to come home; in Malaysia a daughter waits many years for revenge against her hated aunt, but finds instead a family secret so terrible, so shocking that she will never recover from it. And in Nigeria a man waits for justice in a court of law, but the judge may be cleverer than he is . . .

BOOKWORMS WORLD STORIES

English has become an international language, and is used on every continent, in many varieties, for all kinds of purposes. *Bookworms World Stories* are the latest addition to the Oxford Bookworms Library. Their aim is to bring the best of the world's stories to the English language learner, and to celebrate the use of English for storytelling all around the world.

Jennifer Bassett
Series Editor

ACKNOWLEDGEMENTS

The publishers are grateful to the following for permission to adapt and simplify copyright texts:

Tod Collins for *Meeting Susamatekkie*;

Teoh Choon Ean for *The Silk Fan* from *Silverfish New Writing 1* (Silverfishbooks, Kuala Lumpur, 2001);

Peter James for *Down South* (Highly Commended Winner in the 2006 Commonwealth Short Story competition);

Lee Jing-Jing for *Eclipse* from the *Quarterly Literary Review Singapore*, Vol. 9 No. 1 Jan 2010 <http://www.qlrs.com>;

Luke Jorsling for *An Old Wife's Tale* (Highly Commended Winner in the 2005 Commonwealth Short Story competition);

Swapna Kishore for *A Place to Stay* (Highly Commended Winner in the 2005 Commonwealth Short Story competition);

Sylvia McNickle for *The Policy* (Highly Commended Winner in the 2005 Commonwealth Short Story competition);

Elise Moser for *Or Be Killed* (Highly Commended Winner in the 2005 Commonwealth Short Story competition);

Ridjal Noor for *Swamiji's Ring* from *Collateral Damage* (Silverfishbooks, Kuala Lumpur, 2004);

C. J. Onyia for *Anywhere But Here* (Highly Commended Winner in the 2006 Commonwealth Short Story competition);

Kachi A. Ozumba for *The One-Armed Thief* (Regional Winner for Africa in the 2009 Commonwealth Short Story competition);

Sue Seah for *Clean Sheets* (Highly Commended Winner in the 2006 Commonwealth Short Story competition);

Eleanor Verbicky-Todd for *Recycling* (Highly Commended Winner in the 2006 Commonwealth Short Story competition).

OXFORD BOOKWORMS LIBRARY
World Stories

A Time of Waiting
Stories from Around the World

Stage 4 (1400 headwords)

Series Editor: Jennifer Bassett
Founder Editor: Tricia Hedge
Activities Editors: Jennifer Bassett and Christine Lindop

NOTES ON THE ILLUSTRATORS

CHANDRAMOHAN KULKARNI (illustrations on pages 4, 12, 23, 43, 64) was born in 1956 in Pune, Maharashtra, India. He has been a freelance artist for many years, working in book illustration and cover design. He has done almost 5,000 cover designs, and illustrates contemporary literature in Marathi, a local Indian language. His work is shown in exhibitions throughout India.

MESHACK ASARE (illustrations on pages 18, 37, 52, 70) was born in Ghana in 1945. He studied Art, and later Social Anthropology, and was a teacher for many years. He is now a very well-known writer and illustrator of children's books. His books have won numerous awards, including Noma and UNESCO awards, and have been published in many countries.

LACHLAN CREAGH (illustrations on pages 28, 32, 46, 57) was born in Townsville, Queensland, Australia. He studied industrial design for several years, and then took a degree in computer animation. Since then he has created animation and illustration for many computer games. He now also works as an illustrator, and has illustrated many books for children.

RETOLD BY CLARE WEST

A Time of Waiting

Stories from Around the World

OXFORD UNIVERSITY PRESS

OXFORD
UNIVERSITY PRESS

Great Clarendon Street, Oxford, OX2 6DP, United Kingdom

Oxford University Press is a department of the University of Oxford.
It furthers the University's objective of excellence in research, scholarship,
and education by publishing worldwide. Oxford is a registered trade
mark of Oxford University Press in the UK and in certain other countries

ISBN: 978 0 19 479460 2

A complete recording of this Bookworms edition of *A Time of Waiting:
Stories from Around the World* is also available in an audio pack ISBN: 978 0 19 479459 6

Printed in China

Word count (main text): 13,874 words

For more information on the Oxford Bookworms Library,
visit www.oup.com/bookworms

CONTENTS

NOTE ON THE LANGUAGE

There are many varieties of English spoken in the world, and the characters in these stories sometimes use non-standard forms (for example, leaving out auxiliary verbs such as *are* and *is*). This is how the authors of the original stories represented the spoken language that their characters would actually use in real life.

There are also words that are usually only found in other Englishes (for example, *mealie-meal*), and a few words from other languages. All these words are either explained in the stories or in the glossary on page 72.

A Place to Stay

SWAPNA KISHORE

A story from India, retold by Clare West

> *The great cities of India are crowded with people. Many of them are poor; they work long hours and earn just enough to buy some food to eat, and to rent a room to sleep in. Life is hard for them.*
>
> *And life is even harder if, like Lakshmi and her husband Ramu, you live in a shanty town, where any day your house can be pulled down and you are suddenly homeless . . .*

'Is Sharada in? We've come for the room,' Lakshmi said, bright and businesslike, to the young girl at the door.

'Sit. I'll call mother.' The girl walked towards a door off the courtyard, bending backwards to support her swollen belly.

As Lakshmi squatted on the dirty stone floor of the courtyard, she looked around with distaste. In a corner there was a rusty tap, with a pile of unwashed bowls under it; uneaten rice and vegetables, swollen and going bad, floating on a pool of dark, oily water.

Her husband Ramu dropped down on to the floor near her, holding a red hand-towel against his hot, wet forehead.

The lines of tiredness on his face made Lakshmi feel guilty.

He had been pulling heavy women around town on his rickshaw all day. Instead of greeting him with tea at their home in the shanty town, she had gone to meet him after work and made him come here.

'Have they decided? Will it be pulled down?' he asked.

'In a fortnight,' she whispered. 'Someone from the apartments went to the lawyers. Called our shanty town a danger to people's health. The lady I work for at number 206 told me.'

'Why?' he whispered back angrily. 'The people who live in the apartments – most of their servants are from our shanties. And the vegetable sellers. And car cleaning boys.'

Lakshmi had been trying to answer this question since this morning, while washing dirty plates and bowls in the six apartments where she worked.

'Enough poor people nearby, in Trilokpuri, who can work for them instead,' she said.

'You know Sharada well?'

'A bit. Met her while I was buying food. Someone mentioned today that her room is available.'

'With a room here, we can continue the work we've got. Your apartments. My rickshaw. But if we have to move miles away . . .' he whispered.

'Rents will go up around here when everyone hears the news about the shanty town,' Lakshmi added.

They were silent.

'Sharada's daughter is like our Paro,' Ramu said after a while. 'When is Paro coming to stay, to have her baby?'

'January.'

Sharada came out into the courtyard. 'Want to see the room?'

It was three metres by three and a half metres, with a small window. The walls were rough and needed repairing. There was a corner blackened by smoke from cooking fires – the 'kitchen'.

'Toilet's shared – that way,' Sharada pointed.

I'll need a clothesline outside the window, Lakshmi thought. When Paro's had her baby, there'll be many things to wash . . .

'You have to be clean,' said Sharada. 'This is not a shanty.'

Lakshmi felt angry. In her home, bowls shone, clothes were kept in tidy piles. No dust at all. The sacred basil plant outside was green and sweet-smelling – but she'd have to leave that behind. No space here.

'Rent?' asked Ramu.

'One thousand monthly. One month's money now.'

Higher than expected, but we'll manage, thought Lakshmi. Cut out the weekly fish meal. Eat less. Take more jobs to afford oil for lighting the daily lamp in front of the shining figures of the gods.

'Can't you make it cheaper?' Ramu asked.

Sharada looked bored. 'You discuss – it's up to you. Another couple is willing, but they need time to find the first month's money.'

After Sharada went inside, Lakshmi whispered, 'We'll manage. To pay the first month, I'll borrow from the lady at 206 – the other ladies won't lend. And we'll see how much we can get for my jewellery. Maybe we can buy it back later.'

When Sharada came out, Lakshmi took out some dirty notes
and handed them to her.

He nodded, but his eyes were like those of dead fish.

When Sharada came out, Lakshmi took out some dirty notes and handed them to her. 'You'll get the rest on Tuesday while we're moving.'

Sharada's fingers closed tightly around the money. Her eyes shone greedily. She nodded.

Lakshmi and Ramu had reached their home in the shanty town when they remembered his hand-towel. Lakshmi went back for it.

She could hear Sharada's voice through the closed door. 'See! A thousand! You could smell their desperation. They must be from the shanty town – people say it's going to be pulled down in a couple of weeks.'

A man spoke. 'But we need another thousand to pay what the family of Munni's husband are asking. And if our Munni has a daughter instead of a son, they'll want twice as much.'

'We'll find more work and get the money. But they're such greedy people – maybe our daughter would be happier staying here with us. Let's see.'

Work, hope, wait – that's life, Lakshmi told herself, standing outside, wondering whether to knock.

The Silk Fan

TEOH CHOON EAN

A story from Malaysia, retold by Clare West

All families have secrets in their past. Some are surprising, some are sad, some are so dark and shocking that it would be better if they stayed buried for ever.

Lin Lin is going home for the funeral of her uncle Hock Leong. She has a message for her aunt Ah Kim, a very special message, in the shape of a white silk fan . . .

There was a very old sign in gold and black outside the shop, placed over the entrance. For as long as she could remember, it carried the name of her uncle, Hock Leong, in large dull gold letters against the black background. Now two narrow pieces of white paper crossed out the name, informing everyone that there had been a death inside the house.

She stood hesitatingly outside the doorway. It seemed that no one had noticed her arrival. The pavement outside the shop and part of the road were covered with tables, and a lot of people sat around, eating and drinking tea. Although they were talking together, it was hard to hear anything except the loud sad music from a small band of five musicians, playing nearby. It was no wonder that, from a distance, as he turned into Chulia Street from Penang Road, her Indian taxi-driver had thought at first that it was a wedding.

But she knew better. Hock Leong had died. She wanted to think that he had 'passed on', as they would say in the family. No one would say the word 'died' openly. She did not like funerals, but she still had to come.

The silk fan was wrapped in brown paper in her large handbag. The fan was small and round, made of pale white silk, with a handle. It had taken her a long time to find a fan like this, but it was exactly what she wanted.

She had considered every detail of what was about to happen, so many times over the last seven years. She was twenty-one when she started planning, but it had really all started a long, long time ago.

'*You must never forget that Uncle brought you up,*' her mother used to remind her all the time. Her uncle did not have much time for children, but she grew up as part of his family, with his sons. For as long as she could remember, he was always there, replacing the father she had never known.

Just inside the shop, the floor had been cleared to leave space for the coffin and altar, which stood in the centre. Priests dressed in yellow moved around, half speaking, half singing. Joss sticks were burning on the altar. She looked at the end of the coffin, and the large framed photograph of her uncle stared back at her. He was a big, heavy man with a fierce look in his eyes that not even the soft light of the photo could hide. Her mother had been small and pretty and you would not imagine them to be brother and sister, but they were. Her uncle had been very good to her mother. He had taken care of her all her life. He was gentle and soft when he spoke to her. But her mother, Lin Lin remembered, always seemed strangely afraid of her big, strong brother.

'*Uncle, uncle!*' Lin Lin was always calling him, when she was little, wanting him to notice her as often as possible. Now he was gone, and she was left feeling empty, with an uneasy fear of what was going to happen that day.

'*What happened to my father? Did he die? Did he?*'

As a child she was always asking whoever would listen to her. Her mother remained silent, and never talked about Lin Lin's father and why they had to live with her uncle. Lin Lin never knew whether her father was dead or alive. Ah Kim, her uncle's wife, used to hold her arms painfully tight and shake her hard whenever she asked the question, and Lin Lin used to cry.

'*Tell me about my father,*' she begged her aunt, when she was sixteen and too big to be shaken. Ah Kim looked at her with narrowed eyes and laughed, making a thin empty sound. Her aunt was quite pretty, with a wide fair face, but her eyes were hard and she had thin lips.

'*Your mother is an autumn fan,*' said her aunt. Her mother heard Ah Kim and walked away to the back of the house, to her room. Lin Lin heard her mother crying softly. Later, she found out that 'an autumn fan' meant a woman whose husband had left her – like a beautiful silk fan, welcome in the summer heat but of no use in the cold autumn season, and she thought she understood why her mother cried.

Her mother had fallen ill and died. Her unhappy life was

wrapped in the past, and somehow that great sadness was too much to live with. Lin Lin was twenty-one and packed her bags to live with friends. She had to leave because it was impossible to live any longer with Ah Kim after her mother's death.

'Lin Lin!' She looked up from her thoughts as someone called out her name. The man coming towards her wore loose-fitting black mourning clothes. He held out his hands and took hers. Beng was her uncle's eldest son and he looked exactly like his father. Lin Lin and cousin Beng grew up together in this very shophouse, where they had lived upstairs on the first floor.

'We have been wondering whether we should call you again, because you hadn't come.' His welcome sounded sincere, and she gave him a small smile.

She saw that all the family had turned their heads to look at her. She was glad she had remembered to put on a black dress. There seemed to be a pause in the conversation, but this was covered up by the band's loud music.

She noted that her uncle's coffin was placed inside the house to show that he had died there. She knew he had not. Why did they pretend? If he died outside the house, the family would have to receive his body wearing non-mourning clothes, and welcome him, pretending he was alive. When his body was inside, they could then recognize it as a dead body, and go into mourning.

She knew her uncle had died in his other house in Kedah, where he lived with a younger mistress, a woman whom all the family called 'the small wife'. She knew because he no longer lived with Ah Kim. She knew because she had carefully followed her uncle's life even after she left to live on her own.

For so long now she had planned for this moment. This moment when she would meet her aunt, face to face, after her uncle's death. Her eyes searched for Ah Kim among the faces of the many people sitting around the coffin.

Ah Kim had grown old, very much older. She was no longer as pretty as Lin Lin remembered her. Her face was lined, but the hard look and thin lips were still there. This was the woman Lin Lin hated for calling her mother an autumn fan.

Ah Kim turned to Lin Lin, her face empty of expression.

'You have come.' That was all she said, her voice slow and deep.

Lin Lin did not smile at her. Ah Kim had not cried, of course. She was supposed to cry noisily for her dead husband, but Lin Lin could tell by her cold, stony eyes that she would not cry. This was the face that had appeared so often in her worst dreams, these were the thin lips that said *'Your mother is an autumn fan'* again and again.

She had never forgotten because these words showed her what she, Lin Lin, was. She was the child of a woman whose husband had left her. She was the unwanted child of an unknown father. Only the thought of her uncle's goodness to her made her wait patiently all these years. Never in her uncle's lifetime would she come to her aunt as she was doing now.

'Are you alone?' Ah Kim asked and suddenly everybody

was asking her questions. Beng pulled out a chair for her, offering her a place at the table with the family.

Lin Lin had nobody, of course. Because she had lived all her life not knowing who her father was, she was afraid to get close to anyone. She carried her uncle's family name; she knew it was not her father's. She felt ashamed whenever she was asked her name, and the feeling followed her and prevented her making any friends. *Was she alone?* Lin Lin looked angrily at her aunt.

'Why don't you burn some joss sticks for your uncle, on the altar?' said one of the family. 'You are too late to see his face. We covered the coffin this morning.'

Beng had placed a few lighted joss sticks in her hand. The pungent smoke went in her eyes. He pushed her towards the altar, but she would not do it. She gave him back the lighted joss sticks.

'I have come to see Ah Kim,' she told her cousin and walked purposefully towards the old woman. Ah Kim was sitting there, looking straight at her with her eyes of cold stone. Had she, too, been waiting for this moment for all these years, expecting what was to happen?

Lin Lin walked over to her, pulling out something flat, wrapped in brown paper, from her handbag. People had stopped talking, whispering, and eating. Only the yellow-dressed priests continued their singing with half-closed eyes, seemingly unaware of what was happening. And the small band played loudly on.

She threw it onto the table in front of her aunt. Ah Kim looked at it, then lifted her eyes to stare at Lin Lin.

*Lin Lin pulled off the brown paper and placed
the white silk fan in front of her aunt.*

'What is this?' Ah Kim asked in a hard voice, breaking the silence. And even before Lin Lin answered, she could tell by the look on her aunt's face that she already knew. Lin Lin pulled off the brown paper and placed the white silk fan in front of her aunt.

'What is this, Ah Kim?' she asked. And everyone hurried forward to look at the white silk fan on the table. There were so many people around, all dressed in black and dark colours. She was delighted that she would do what she had to do in front of so many. Her aunt would be deeply, deeply, ashamed.

When the old woman did not reply and sat looking at the fan without moving, Lin Lin moved closer to her. Her face was very near those thin lips that replayed so often in her most frightening dreams.

'It's a fan, can't you see?' she said. 'You called my mother an autumn fan, you bad heartless woman. You broke her heart.' She paused for breath, her own face showing her pain, forgetting that she was at a funeral.

'Look at this fan, Ah Kim. I bought this for you, to remind you,' she continued, 'because it was not my mother who was the autumn fan, it was you!'

There were gasps from the family, followed by some talking. An ugly sound that was laughter was heard, and Lin Lin realized it was coming from herself. 'My uncle left you for another woman. You're pretending he died inside the house. You are the autumn fan after all! You should know how it feels!'

But when Lin Lin looked into the face of her aunt, it was

not an ashamed or a guilty face that stared back at her. The old woman stood up and took hold of her niece's arms. Lin Lin could not believe that after so many years, her aunt was shaking her violently, just like when she was a child.

'Stupid, stupid girl!' Ah Kim whispered angrily at her. 'In front of your dead uncle, you do this to me?' Then she threw back her head and laughed a deep, ugly laugh, her hands still holding Lin Lin's arms tightly.

'Stupid, stupid girl!' she repeated, her voice louder this time. 'I tried to protect you, to prevent you from finding out, by calling her an autumn fan. The truth is worse than that, you stupid, stupid girl! Now I have to let you know!'

'What is there to know?' Lin Lin asked. The uneasy fear she had lived with all her life was giving her a tight feeling in her chest. Ah Kim let her go suddenly, making Lin Lin fall backwards a step or two. The dark eyes looked deep into hers, and the voice became louder and higher.

'Your uncle was your natural father. Now you know.'

The silence that followed was deafening. Even the priests stopped singing and the funeral band paused in the middle of their playing. The seconds seemed unbelievably long, like all the years of her life rolled into one. Lin Lin felt the darkness rise, wrapping round her as she fell forward, knocking the silk fan off the table.

The silk fan fell noisily, unheard and unnoticed, onto the floor.

Meeting Susamatekkie

TOD COLLINS

A story from South Africa, retold by Clare West

In the mountains of Lesotho, the local people live a simple life, looking after their animals, and following the pattern of the seasons. But there are also visitors, who come from the cities to walk and climb, and enjoy the beauty of the mountains.

The narrator of this story is a man from the city, and as he walks through the mountains, he meets a young Basutho man . . .

'What's your name?'

'Susamatekkie.'

'And your family name?'

'Gumede.'

'My name is Tod, family name Collins.'

The young Basutho was taller than me and his teeth were shining white, not my sort of yellowish-white. A grey blanket hung from his neck and shoulders, and he wore rubber boots. When he bent down to calm one of his growling dogs, his blanket opened a little, and I could see that he was wearing a pair of shorts, with no shirt. All my clothes were made of the latest modern materials, especially made for mountain-climbing by well-known clothing companies.

When we'd first met, I'd asked if he spoke any isiZulu. In this distant part of Lesotho, some of the boys and men who travel around with their animals can speak it.

He was in his mid-twenties, and had been living in this valley, between the square-topped mountain known as Thaba Koto and the triangle-shaped Walker's Peak, for about fifteen years. I had walked here from the Sani Pass, a road through the mountains a couple of days away.

'Is it OK for me to sleep here?' I asked him. We were on a flat bit of ground on the edge of the stream.

'*Eeeeh,*' he said. Yes. It sounded like the way Australians in Darwin say 'air'.

'But it'll be cold!' he continued, with a laugh. 'This is a sheltered place and the sun rises late.'

I told him I had a tent to sleep in and a stove for cooking food and making hot drinks. He nodded, then asked where I was from. When I told him, a smile came over his face and he asked why I was carrying a backpack and sleeping in a tent among these *ntabas*, the mountains high above us.

I tried to explain that some of us like to get away from things which worry and annoy us – telephones and people and their animals' problems.

'Oh,' he said, 'I have a problem with my cattle too. I did have sixteen but my bull died.'

I asked how his cows would get calves next year.

He didn't seem to know, and stared into the distance. 'I'll ask at Thamathu village when I buy my mealie-meal there next month. Somebody may have a bull that I can use.'

We were silent for a while, and when it seemed that he

was going to walk away, I asked, 'Do you eat mealie-meal every day?'

'*Eeeeh*, but sometimes the dogs kill a wild animal and that means I can eat meat. We ate the bull's meat for a long time. And sometimes when a cow has her calf, I get the afterbirth before she eats it herself, and that is excellent.'

From my backpack I pulled out an orange and a Jungle Energy Bar. He put down his stick, and accepted them. After a moment he put them on the ground too, then took my hand with both of his and shook it very enthusiastically. His eyes were filled with delight and his perfect teeth shone.

During our conversation, his cattle had moved slowly down the valley to the place where he kept them at night, close to his small stone house. As he ran down the valley towards them, he shouted at the top of his voice.

'. . . *iswidi* . . . *iwolintshi* . . .' were two words that I understood (sweet, orange), and from much further down the valley his neighbour shouted something back.

I saw Susamatekkie the next morning while I was drinking coffee outside the tent. The ground was white and hard after an extremely cold night. He was driving his cattle up the valley – they would stay there for the day, eating what grass they could find. He didn't even have a hat to keep his head warm.

'Are you going home now?' he asked.

'Yes, I should be home by night-time.'

'Will you come here again?'

'Yes, certainly, I'll come again before I get too old,' I replied.

I saw Susamatekkie the next morning while I was drinking coffee outside the tent.

'Could I visit you if I came to Underberg?'

'Yes, indeed, Susamatekkie, you must come!'

'Well, do you think you could arrange for me to ride in a motor car? That's something I would like to do before I become old.'

'Yes, I could arrange that,' I replied in wonder, then added, 'What will you do after you have taken your cattle up the valley now?'

From the way he looked at me, I could see he thought I was a bit stupid. 'I will go back to my house and wait until it is time to bring them back this evening,' he said.

That was a few months ago, in May. We are now experiencing one of the coldest winters for more than thirty years. The snows have fallen very heavily.

After two weeks the south-facing mountain sides and valleys are still thickly covered. Thaba Koto, Wilson's Peak and the nearby mountain tops and valleys are particularly wonderful to look at. We can see them from our house in Underberg. The snow must be at least waist deep up there. Crowds of people from the cities have come in their fast, modern motor cars to touch the snow, play in it, and take photos with digital cameras.

AUTHOR'S NOTE

This story won the snapshot category of the 2007 True Stories of KwaZulu-Natal Competition, and I received the prize of 2000 South African Rand. I went back to Susamatekkie's home and found him there. I showed him the story in print (which he couldn't read) and also his photograph, which I had included with the story. He was delighted with his picture. Then I gave him a handful of ten hundred-Rand notes, which was half the prize money. He didn't seem very excited by this, so I told him that I would take it to the trading store in Thamathu village, and he could buy things there with the money.

I have a good friend who lives in Thamathu, and he is friendly with the storekeeper. My friend will keep an eye on Susamatekkie's money, and the storekeeper now has a photo of Susamatekkie, so that he is the only person who can use this money to buy things.

Clean Sheets

SUE SEAH

A story from Singapore, retold by Clare West

Cleaning, changing the bed, washing the sheets – ordinary, everyday tasks that have no special meaning. But sometimes even ordinary things can tell a story. Words are not needed; only actions.

A husband watches as his wife does ordinary, everyday things in their home. But what is really happening here?

She takes all the sheets to the Laundromat. They will be washed and dried there in the big machines lined up in a row. She leaves the sheets there and comes back wearing a new dress. She bought it on her way home. It's in light sand-coloured material. Sensible. Washable. It has no scent of its own, but a smell of newness which tells you it has not been worn and washed. A scent which you can only breathe in if you are close enough. From a distance, she tells me she wants to start her life again, to make a clean beginning. She's not leaving to think things through; she has already straightened them all out in her head.

Quietly, she sweeps the apartment, cleans the bathroom, and removes every one of her long hairs from the floor and the furniture. Next, she takes out her brown suitcase and her clothes, and places them on the bed. One by one she lays the pieces carefully in the case. There isn't much to pack. She has made some trips to the thrift store recently, taking plastic bags with her each time. I suddenly realize that she has been clearing out her clothes over the past weeks. Then she walks to the bathroom to collect her things.

I'm sitting on the sofa, looking at her suitcase on the bed.

'I guess this is it,' I say.

She continues to pack – her comb, toothbrush, make-up, her bottle of perfume. There is a rustling sound as she puts her towels, still wet from her morning wash, into a plastic bag. After that, she goes to the kitchen and gets her cup.

'You gave those clothes away, to the thrift store,' I say. I don't know what else to say. Those were things that I bought or chose for her.

I look at her case. Packing is strange. We packed when we went on trips. We packed when we moved from one apartment to another. Now the case contains only things that belong to her, things she has bought on her own, without telling me or asking my advice.

The clothes are laid in neat, rectangular piles. They are about to make a journey which I am not allowed to go on. She comes over and closes the lock. For a long while she sits on the bed, her back towards me. I cannot see her face, but it doesn't matter. I know she wants me to see her hair. It is nothing special, but its scent is my first awareness in the morning, and my last as I close my eyes at night.

Then she stands up. The mattress rises with her, but quickly returns to its usual flatness. On the sheetless bed

The clothes are laid in neat, rectangular piles. They are about to make a journey which I am not allowed to go on.

there is no sign of where she was sitting. She takes her case and makes her way to the door. And still, I cannot see her face – and whether there are tears in her eyes.

'Remember to collect the clean sheets,' she says, 'they will be ready at two o'clock.'

She puts on her shoes and walks out. They are new shoes, just like the clothes she is wearing. Shoes she has bought during her trip out in the morning, shoes that will go some place I will never know.

I look around our apartment, my apartment now. It is perfectly clean and tidy. Nothing has been left behind, no clothes, not a single hair. Not even a breath of scent in the air. She did not wear perfume that day.

I look at the bed. I think of the sheets going round and round inside the washing machine at the Laundromat. It is washing even the memory of her out of the sheets. There is a hole in one of them. I cannot remember how the hole was made, but it has become bigger each time the sheet is used. It needed mending some time ago. It's too late for that now.

Or Be Killed

ELISE MOSER

A story from Canada, retold by Clare West

Polar bears live and hunt in the snow and ice of northern Canada. They are powerful and dangerous animals, and have no enemies – except, of course, human beings, who take their land, and hunt and kill them.

In the wild there is only one law among animals – kill, or be killed. Cam knows that, as she was once a hunter herself . . .

When Cam first saw them, they looked like white against white, moving past walls of snow shining in the early light. Then they became actual figures. A mother polar bear and two cubs. The adult's beautiful neck was waving as she smelt the air. Then the bear turned, and Cam saw the black nose and dark eyes. And in an electric moment she saw the bear see her too – and knew she was standing too close.

The hair on Cam's neck stood on end. She looked around her, at the frozen piles of rubbish from people's kitchens and houses. Maybe she could hide somewhere here, although she knew the bear would smell her. And her breath rose like white smoke in the cold air, making a flag that the bear would certainly see. The clear air was still so cold, this early in the spring, that it felt like a trap, ready to close around her.

Cam's father had been a hunter. He had often taken her with him on hunting trips. She remembered the cloud of hot air rising from the opened stomach of a freshly killed animal. She imagined the heat of her own insides rushing out of her.

'I only kill what I can eat,' her father used to say proudly. 'It's a law of nature.'

And Cam remembered seeing the bloody meat of the dead animal and looking forward to eating it.

The mother bear had pushed her young ones behind her, protecting them lovingly. She faced Cam across the snow-covered distance less than a hundred and fifty metres away, and growled.

Cam heard the low, threatening sound, and it made her feel cold to the bone. She felt sadness rise inside her. It had been stupid of her to come out to this place alone, with no weapon. She knew that bears often came here, looking for food among the piles of garbage. She knew that, and still she had come. Restlessness had driven her from the house, and she had wanted to walk. But she had been too busy with her thoughts to notice that she was entering the garbage area. And now here she was, right in the middle of the rows of frozen rubbish.

Nearby, the tops of the garbage piles were hidden by shining snow, which had built up over months of hard dark winter. Cam looked wildly around but she couldn't see any weapons she could possibly use. A loose chair leg, perhaps, that she could throw. A last desperate attempt to stop 250 kilos of angry bear coming any closer. Cam's heart was beating fast in her chest. She could feel her own blood rushing through her ears, and it deafened her.

Slowly, she took a step backward. The bear moved forward, hot bear breath in a cloud around her head. Cam saw how loose the bear's skin was on her bones. She must be hungry, her cubs must be hungry. At the edge of Cam's view, they were searching fruitlessly among the frozen garbage. Rubbish that had been spreading, little by little, since long before they were born, on the land where bears had lived for centuries. Rubbish that was poisoning the huge hunting ground where the bears had once had no enemies, only plenty of food.

Now, Cam knew, the climate was too warm for seawater to freeze as much as it used to, so there was less and less pack ice. Polar bears hunt for their food over the pack ice, which meant that now they couldn't find enough food. So here they were, driven by need – because of human beings.

In spite of her fear, Cam felt both ashamed and sorry. Suddenly the mother bear, once a fierce and proud hunter, was now just any animal, searching through garbage for bits of old food.

The bear put her head down and began to move forward. Cam held her breath and tried to keep calm. She was weak, had only two legs, and could not run as fast as her hunter. The bear stopped and growled loudly at her, a rough, angry sound. Cam could see that her fur was very thin in places. Was this natural, or caused by hunger?

In her mind's eye, she saw the first animal she had killed

*Cam knelt down in the snow and began to take off
the scarf around her neck.*

as a hunter years ago. And she remembered how certain she had been that it was right for some animals to die because other animals needed them as food. She saw the great, clean white area of windswept ice, out of which this huge, beautiful animal had appeared, driven by a mother's need to find food for her young.

Then Cam felt herself, bright hot blood rushing through the red meat of her body. She knelt down in the snow and began to take off the scarf around her neck.

Down South

PETER JAMES

A story from Australia, retold by Clare West

On the great surf beaches of Australia, surfers ride their boards, always searching for a bigger, better wave.

Mike and Ben are driving down a rocky track to a surf beach far from anywhere on the cold, southern coast of Victoria. They love the danger of the battle with wind and water, and are experienced surfers, ready for anything that the sea can throw at them . . .

'That's the strange thing,' Mike says. 'The other people in the show are believable. The one that doesn't work is Jerry Seinfeld himself.'

'What, are you serious?' Ben says, putting on a New York accent.

'Seinfeld can't act. It's a kind of stand-up comedy routine for him. He forgets he's in a TV show.'

'So you don't like the show?'

'No, I like the show, I just don't like Jerry.'

'Well, Jerry *is* the show. If you don't like Jerry, you don't like the show.'

Their Land Rover is powerful, but the road is difficult, and the car's engine works extra hard. The back wheels slip sideways and mud shoots out across the bushes on either side. Rain is falling heavily, and the regular sound of the windscreen wipers is like the start of a Pink Floyd song. It's warm inside the car. It's icy outside.

'My wetsuit's wet,' Mike says, miserably. 'I hate getting into wet wetties.'

'Everyone hates getting into wet wetties,' Ben tells him.

'Funny how you hate it so much, but it's only a few minutes of being in the wet wettie, and then you're in the water anyway.'

'But if I could choose, I'd rather get into a dry wetsuit, then get wet,' says Ben, happy at the thought of his bone dry wetsuit.

'Get out and open the gate,' Mike says angrily.

'How much further, do you think? We must be close now,' Ben says, pulling off his muddy boots and placing his feet over the heater on the dashboard.

'Your feet stink!' says Mike.

The car pushes its way up the narrow beach road and around a tight bend. Weatherbeaten bushes scratch at both sides, filling the car with a screaming noise, as the ocean finally shows itself.

'Whoa! Plenty of swell!' Ben says. 'Got to be – six to eight feet?'

'Bigger, I'd say,' says Mike excitedly. 'That's a long way down there.'

'Do we walk from here?'

'Suppose.'

In the next ten minutes they move fast, getting boards out

Standing there in wetsuits on the edge of the shore,
they see the waves push up the sand toward them.

of covers and throwing clothes wildly into the back seat, as they prepare for their battle with wind and water.

'AAARGH!' Mike shouts noisily as he pushes a leg unwillingly into the cold wet wetsuit.

They make their way along the narrow path towards the sea. It's only now that they realize the waves are considerably bigger than they first thought. The cold sand begins stealing the life from their toes, turning their feet into blocks of ice.

'How big?' Ben says, sounding unconfident.

'Big enough. How do we get out there?'

All excitement has gone now, as they reach the shore. The ocean is grey and threatening. The wind blows past their ears angrily, racing out to sea to meet the huge waves breaking slowly in front of them. The ocean looks more alive than they feel. They are small and unimportant. There is danger in the air.

But they can't go back now. Standing there in wetsuits on the edge of the shore, they see the waves push up the sand toward them, pulling at their feet.

Ben's eyes search the first hundred metres of water for a way out.

'Through there, I think,' he says.

'This doesn't look like much fun,' says Mike.

'A good beating won't hurt us.'

Ben takes a step forward, a step he can't take back. Another step and a wave pushes past. He throws himself forward, lands on his board, and paddles fast.

Mike stares out to sea. Something's not right. The sky is grey, the water is grey, his wet wetsuit is making him shiver.

He takes a step, then another, then throws himself forward and lands on his board, pushing his way through the water behind Ben. Icy salt water enters his wetsuit, and the ocean heaves with delight.

An Old Wife's Tale

LUKE JORSLING

A story from Trinidad, retold by Clare West

*Fishermen's wives are used to waiting –
waiting for the fishing boats to come back to
shore, waiting for the sound of footsteps
returning home. The sea is a dangerous place,
and it is hard not to worry.*

*All they can do is wait and hope – and look
for signs of good luck wherever they can . . .*

At first, the old woman had not really noticed it, the green grasshopper that flew past her and into the house. She was standing at the open window, looking out. Night had fallen on the seashore. Only a little pale light hung in the western sky, showing where the sun had gone down.

She watched the empty boats moving up and down in the shallow water by the beach. The tide was slowly rising. All the other fishermen had returned home for the evening. Only her husband's boat had not come in yet.

She left the window open and sat down at the dining table to wait. An oil lamp burned brightly on the table, while two empty drinking glasses shone with little points of light, like the starlit sky over the beach.

Her husband would normally be home by now, sitting at the other end of the table. He would tell her all about his adventures at sea that day. Meanwhile, they would eat the fish he had caught and brought home and she had cooked for their supper.

He would tell her proudly how far out to sea he had gone. Further out than any of the younger fishermen dared to go, because they were afraid they would be caught fishing in Venezuelan waters and would end up in a Venezuelan prison. They were even more afraid of meeting pirates who wanted to steal the engines from their boats.

But he knew the sea better than the Venezuelans or the pirates, he would tell her, so he could make his boat go faster than any of them.

'You're too big-headed,' she would smile and tell him then.

'Too big-headed,' she cried now, although he wasn't there to hear her, 'to even carry a lamp on your boat. If you were robbed of your engine and left in your boat, out there on the sea all night, pushed this way and that by the wind and the waves, what would you do? If you carried a lamp, a passing big ship would see you and pick you up and not run over you.'

Through her tears, she saw the green grasshopper on the wall. A house lizard, waving its tail from side to side to confuse the grasshopper, was slowly getting closer to it. The lizard was within attacking distance when the grasshopper flew away, jumping on and off the walls, into the lampshade, and finally landing on the table.

It is said that if a green grasshopper flies into your home at night and you put a glass over it and let it go in the

The grasshopper flew away, jumping on and off the walls, into the lampshade, and finally landing on the table.

morning, you will have good luck and become rich. The old woman took an empty glass and put it down on the table over the green grasshopper.

And sure enough, the next morning she lifted the glass, and the green grasshopper jumped up and in a golden stream of morning light flew out of the door. It flew past her husband, who stood in the doorway with a sea-salt smile on his face and a rich basket of fish in his arms.

She lifted her head from her arms that rested on the table, and looked around. The strong morning light was painful on her eyes. Her husband still hadn't come home. What she had seen was only a dream. She was angry with herself. How could she fall asleep at a time like this? She supposed she had slept all night.

She saw the green grasshopper still inside the glass on the table. She lifted the glass. The grasshopper remained still. She gently touched its wings. Very slowly it moved a little way away, then was still again. Suddenly its wings opened out and it was off, flying in a beautiful curving line out of the open window. And was gone.

Swamiji's Ring

RIDJAL NOOR

A story from Malaysia, retold by Clare West

A fortune-teller can use magic to tell you what will happen to you in the future. That's what some people believe. Other people think that it is all nonsense, just silly superstition.

Rahul certainly does not believe in magic or fortune-tellers or things of that kind. What nonsense, he tells his mother. Unfortunately, his mother has other ideas . . .

His mother came back from the visit visibly excited and hopeful.

'Swamiji has given me something that will solve all your troubles,' she cried, the moment she stepped into the house. Rahul looked up from the magazine at her, ready to be cautious. She was wearing a light green sari with a purple top, which was wet under her arms. The hair round her face also looked wet and lay flat on her forehead.

She searched through her bag and brought out a flat, square packet. 'Here,' she said, passing it to him. 'Open it!'

Rahul unwrapped the paper. There was a metal ring inside the packet.

'Swamiji says, put on this ring and you will find success in whatever you do. Now, you will have no trouble getting a job, no? Just wear the ring and good fortune will be with you,' his mother cried, smiling proudly at him.

Rahul held the ring between his thumb and first finger. It was thin and light, but felt heavy with all the hope that his mother had placed on it. These fortune-tellers make me angry, Rahul thought to himself.

In the past, he had tried to make his mother understand that she was being foolish, believing in all this silly superstition, but she would never listen to him.

'You are still young and you don't know anything,' she had once told him. 'What would you know about the ways of the world? Wait until you have experience of life, like me!' She shook her head at him in an annoying way and smiled her motherly smile.

At first, he had explained and argued, refusing to believe in these superstitions and wanting her to see the truth. But soon he found that it was easier to say nothing when his mother talked about Swamiji and his magic, because there seemed to be no way of making her think differently. She was sure that the stupid magic worked, and in the end he was happy to let her believe that.

That Friday, Rahul had an interview for an engineering job with an important international company. He wore his dark blue trousers with a light blue shirt and brushed his hair back neatly.

He had been looking for a job for the past six months, but with no success. There had been the occasional interview, always followed by the polite letter saying 'No', but none of the interviews had promised a job with a better future than this one. Rahul hoped against hope that he would do well in the interview.

His mother had gone out early in the morning to pray for his success, and she returned in time to speak to Rahul before the interview. There was the matter of the ring.

'Where is the ring, Rahul?' she asked, noticing that he was not wearing it.

'In my pocket, Ma. Don't worry. I'll put it on later,' he said, thinking up a quick lie. He had not meant to use the ring or its so-called 'magic' at all. In fact, at that very moment, Rahul was worriedly trying to remember where he had last put the ring down.

'Don't lie,' his mother told him, frowning. 'You left it on the table last night and forgot all about it.' She took it out of her sari and placed it in his hand.

'Don't be difficult, dear. Put it on,' she said, with a persuasive smile.

Rahul sighed and put the ring on the first finger of his left hand, to please his mother. 'There. Are you happy now?' he said.

'Now, don't be like that,' his mother said. 'Swamiji's magic will help you, now that you're wearing the ring. Don't be afraid or worried. You will certainly do well.'

He had clearly forgotten about the ring after that.

He was one of the first to arrive for the interview. The interviewer was a grey-haired man with glasses and a grey beard, who was the head of the company. He seemed very interested in Rahul's education and training, and in his replies to the questions thrown at him. At the end of an hour-long interview, the grey-haired man got up from his seat and reached over to shake Rahul's hand.

'Well done, young man,' he said, with a smile. 'I very much like what I've seen and heard from you so far. I believe this company would do well to have someone as intelligent and enthusiastic as you. You've got the job.'

Rahul rose from his seat and shook the man's hand warmly. 'Thank you, sir. Thank you very much. You won't be disappointed.'

They were smiling at each other and Rahul was delighted at the success of the interview. At that moment, he caught sight of the ring on his finger, and something turned over in his stomach.

'You've got the job?' his mother cried out loud, when he arrived home.

'Yes, but—' Rahul started to say.

'Oh, you see, I told you! Ah, thank you, Swamiji!' his mother was saying. 'Tomorrow, Rahul, you will follow me to Swamiji's house and we will take him presents, to show how grateful we are for his help. What a lucky ring, indeed!'

'Now, see here, Ma! It's not—' Rahul tried to say.

'Ah, I told you! I told you! Swamiji's magic always works. People come to him from all over the country. Not only Hindu, no. Even Muslims and Christians, people who pray to different gods, they come to see Swamiji to ask for help and advice,' his mother said, laughing.

'Oh, you see, I told you! Ah, thank you, Swamiji!'
his mother said. 'What a lucky ring, indeed!'

Rahul pulled the ring off his finger and threw it to the ground.

His mother gasped in shock.

'Now, see here, Ma! No lucky ring, no magic! I got this job because of all I've done. A good education and intelligence. None of this silly superstitious nonsense! No Swamiji! The ring was not the reason I got the job! Why does he get thanks for something he was never even a part of?'

His mother did not reply. She bent to pick up the ring, and when she stood up again, he could see her eyes filling with tears. Silently, she put the ring inside her sari and brushed her tears away with one hand.

'Please, Ma . . .' he said. He knew she would start crying, to try and soften him and make him give in to her. He had expected this.

'No, no, Rahul. You are a big man now, with big ideas. And very clever. No need for stupid superstition or magic. What good is a silly ring or Swamiji to you? Soon, even this old woman is no good to you any more.'

And she brushed her eyes again with the back of her hand and turned to go to the kitchen to prepare dinner, leaving Rahul to search for the right words to mend the moment.

The Policy

SYLVIA McNICKLE

A story from Australia, retold by Clare West

*It is sensible to take out an insurance policy.
Who knows what lies around the corner for
any of us? But if you have insurance, at least
the insurance company will pay you money if
you have an accident, or will pay your family
if you are unfortunate enough to die.*

*Arnold Snell is a sensible man; he believes
in planning for the future. However, his plans
are not quite the same as other people's . . .*

Arnold Snell, licensed butcher, practised rolling a cigarette without using the first finger of his left hand. Bending it forwards and holding it still while the other fingers worked, he spread out tobacco onto the paper, rolled it up neatly and licked the edge of the paper. No problem.

He lit the cigarette and narrowed his eyes against the smoke, as he read through the policy one more time. There it was, in black and white. Thirty thousand dollars if he lost a finger. The company would pay out more for other, larger parts of his body, but Arnold wasn't prepared to lose any of those.

A finger, however, was different – he could manage without that. And thirty thousand dollars would set him free.

'I'd really like to buy fillet, Mr Snell,'
Mrs Prentice told him every week.

Free of hindquarters, forequarters, sausages, and mince. Free of Mrs Prentice's weekly visit to buy a kilogram of topside steak and to complain about her teeth.

'I'd really like to buy fillet, Mr Snell,' she told him every week. 'With my false teeth, it would be so much easier to eat. But who can afford it at these prices?'

'Why doesn't she either grow new teeth, or drop dead?' Arnold used to think crossly. He didn't even eat fillet steak himself. It was the cheaper cuts of meat that he took home to Marge in the evenings – whatever his customers hadn't bought that day.

Marge. A slow smile spread across his face. He'd be free of Marge. He supposed he'd once had a reason for marrying her, but it was so long ago that he'd forgotten what it was. They had no children, which didn't come as any surprise to Arnold. Marge had never enjoyed what she called 'that sort of thing'.

'And anyway,' she added when they discussed it, 'the smell of another body close to mine makes me feel sick.'

Marge was deeply worried about Arnold's refusal to go to church. She herself went every week.

'What if something happened to you, and you're not at peace with God? You haven't confessed to a priest for thirty years, not since before we were married.'

Arnold argued that, thanks to her, he had nothing to confess. Well, thirty thousand dollars would change all that. Maybe he'd go to a casino and play cards for money, or drink whisky from a bottle, the way they did in Western movies. He had a further thought and his heart beat faster.

Maybe he'd visit a woman in town, and pay to get what Marge wouldn't give him.

Arnold found it difficult to hide his delight. He wondered if Marge would miss him. Possibly. Maybe he'd send her a postcard from Turkey or Lapland. Or maybe he wouldn't. Sometimes a clean cut was best. A clean cut.

Arnold laughed quietly and made an appointment with himself. 10 a.m. tomorrow, St Patrick's Day. Perhaps St Patrick was smiling on him. He felt strangely lucky.

Irish people all round the world celebrate St Patrick's Day, and although neither Arnold nor Marge had any Irish family at all, she liked to join in the happiness of the occasion. So, once a year, she brought out the green tablecloth with Irish designs sewn all round the edges.

'Such a bright touch if a visitor happens to call in,' she said to herself as she laid it over the table. 'And if I'm not mistaken, there are footsteps on the front steps right now.'

It was a young policeman, who looked very serious. He refused Marge's offer of a cup of green tea. 'I have bad news,' he said. 'Perhaps you'd like to sit down?'

Arnold's death was quite simple really. At 10 a.m. he had been about to cut off his finger, as he had planned. But when Mrs Prentice entered the shop unexpectedly, he lost his concentration and accidentally cut off the whole of his left hand. He bled to death before you could say 'top-side steak'. Mrs Prentice was taken to hospital, suffering from shock.

Marge watched thoughtfully as the police car drove away. She was a widow, and she felt delighted at this sudden rise in her social importance. She had never liked appearing in public with Arnold anyway – even after he had taken a shower, dogs used to follow them around.

How fortunate that Arnold had an insurance policy! Two hundred thousand dollars would go a long way towards helping her forget her sadness at his death. Perhaps she would go on a trip, somewhere quiet and far away with palm trees and beach umbrellas. Marge felt sure that Arnold would advise it.

Anywhere But Here

C. J. ONYIA

A story from Nigeria, retold by Clare West

Container ships are ugly things. The ships are piled high with containers, huge metal boxes carrying anything from furniture to washing machines to computers.

Containers are not designed to transport humans, and no one would choose to make a long sea voyage inside a container – unless they were desperate . . .

Two months ago in a flat in the centre of town, I met Calestas for the first time. He was a third year engineering student from the University of Benin. We found we had similar tastes in music, films, and women. Another thing we had in common was that he had just been refused a Schengen visa for the third time, so he had no chance of visiting any of the fifteen countries in Europe that recognize this visa. And my name had failed to appear in the last four green card lotteries, which meant I couldn't get permission to go and live in the United States.

We talked about all this and decided that 'Nigeria no be am' – there was no future for us in Nigeria, none at all.

Ade was a man who worked at the docks – his job was to check workers in and out of the docks when ships were being loaded. He greeted Calestas like an old friend, and they went off to have a private discussion. Then Calestas pushed some money into my hand, and ordered me to go and buy as much bread and tinned fish as I could.

There was another man, called Kazim, who got involved. I never really knew what part he was supposed to play in the plan, because after the accident he was never mentioned again. So there were the four of us.

Ade arranged everything. One night we met him at the docks, and ended up hiding in a fourteen-foot container, which was half full of boxes of office equipment. It was loaded on to a big container ship sailing to Calais in France – at least, that's where we thought we were going.

Ade's information was that we were on our way to France, with no stops, and we would spend about eleven days at sea. But by the fifth day, we had no food left and our drinking water was dangerously low. We managed to cut an opening at one end of the container, but the hole was only large enough for a child or a small man to get through. Luckily, Kazim was quite small, so we sent him out.

We soon depended completely on him for our food. He was like an animal bringing back food to its young, pushing his thin body in and out through the opening. The first night he came back with some tins of vegetables, but then he started to stay out longer and longer. More than once he returned empty-handed, telling us that all the cupboards were locked up and he couldn't find any food.

Calestas and Ade were beginning to suspect that something was wrong. One night, after Kazim had left, they

The stupid man thought he could escape by jumping
on top of one of the largest containers.

sat by the hole and managed to widen it a little more, until with great difficulty we were able to get through. Once we were out in the open, Ade discovered about thirty empty tins which had contained fish and vegetables, hidden under an old coat near our container. Kazim, for whatever reason, had been lying to us.

We waited silently in the shadows for his return. When he appeared, we chased him round the containers, which were piled dangerously on top of each other, and finally trapped him in a corner. He knew we would beat him if we caught him, but the stupid man thought he could escape by jumping on top of one of the largest containers. In his fear and excitement, he slipped, and disappeared over the side of the ship into the sea.

We heard shouts and running feet. I suppose someone saw him fall or heard him hit the water. But there was no sign of his body in the sea.

There and then we made a promise to tell the truth. Illegal immigration is one thing, killing someone is another.

The three of us had our hands tied and we were locked up in a room together. The ship's officers couldn't agree what to do with us.

We were at sea for two more days and then, when the ship arrived at Rotterdam, in the Netherlands, they hurried us off the ship. It was bitterly cold in Rotterdam.

We were handed over to the immigration officer, who was the only person we met who spoke English. We were kept there for four days at an immigration centre, then we were taken to the train station by the police and sent to

Amsterdam. There we were put on a plane at the airport. Five and a half hours later we landed at Murtala Muhammed Airport in Lagos.

Calestas is back at university. Ade later got a job as a driver for a company in Lagos. And me? Well, I watch the ships come in, down at the docks. I'd rather be anywhere but here.

Recycling

ELEANOR VERBICKY-TODD

A story from Canada, retold by Clare West

Millions of garbage bins are emptied every day around the world. Why do we throw so much away? Can't some of it be used again? What's rubbish to one person might be something useful to another person.

Recycling is popular today – clothes, glass, paper, all kinds of things can be recycled. And sometimes recycling can have unexpected effects, as Judith discovers . . .

Judith stood in front of the kitchen window, washing last night's dishes, just as she did every morning. Each day her feet made a deeper mark on the worn floor. Through the thin curtain on the window, she saw that it was a grey winter morning. But no snow had fallen. In the yard there were just a few piles of old snow, which had hardened into dull white ice.

The window looked white round the edges. She would need her coat when she took the garbage down to the bins later. Her breath would make an icy fog, and her toes would feel the bite of winter inside her thin wool slippers.

She shivered, and let her hands stay in the warm dishwater, rubbing the dinner plate slowly with the cloth, spending longer than necessary on the water glass, and washing the knife and fork again and again.

Out of the corner of her eye, she noticed something moving outside, at the far end of the garden. It was a man, wearing a long brown coat and a black baseball cap. His face was hidden behind a thick brown beard.

Judith stood completely still. Was he looking for things to steal? An unlocked window to climb through?

The man lifted the lid of one of her garbage bins and looked inside, then did the same to the second bin. From the third, he pulled out an old radio Judith had thrown away, and put it inside a black leather suitcase he was carrying. The case was a nice piece of luggage, perhaps even by a well-known designer, Judith thought. She was really surprised to see what valuable things people throw away. After putting the lid back on the bin, the man walked unhurriedly away.

Judith felt a little uncomfortable at seeing a vagrant in her tidy, well-organized neighbourhood, but he wasn't bothering anyone. In a way, she told herself, he was being very helpful to people, by recycling things they no longer wanted. He was doing a useful job.

The next morning, she looked in her closet and found the shoebox full of neckties that Richard had left behind. She supposed the reason he hadn't taken them was that they were presents from her. All of them were silk, and very expensive. Putting on her coat, which was hanging near the back door, she went into the garden, taking small steps in her loose-fitting slippers. She placed the box of ties on one of the garbage bins.

*From the third garbage bin, the man pulled out
an old radio Judith had thrown away.*

She returned to the kitchen and washed the dishes from the night before, watching for the vagrant through the thin curtain. He appeared, carrying his black suitcase. When he put the box of ties into his bag, she felt a sense of relief, like a gentle rain falling in the back of her mind.

The next day, Judith went out to the garbage bins again, and put into one of them a small painting. Richard had given it to her after twenty years of marriage, on the date of their wedding.

The following morning, she put out their wedding photo, in its silver frame.

Finally, she placed her wedding ring in a small box and left it in a bin. She didn't see the man that morning, but in the evening she checked the garbage bin and saw that the ring was gone. She let out a long slow breath, and the frown that she had worn for months disappeared.

The man's suitcase was sitting on top of one of the bins. It was a fine-looking leather bag. He didn't need it any more, she supposed. After selling her ring and the other things she'd left, he would eat well for a while.

A light snow began to fall, giving the back garden and the suitcase a soft white covering. She slid her fingers through the handle of the bag, and carried it into the house.

Eclipse

LEE JING-JING

(

A story from Singapore, retold by Clare West

Illness changes everything. It changes your daily routine, it changes how you live, how you think, how you look at the world. But there is one thing it doesn't change – love.

Will and Elise are making a long and painful journey. But they are making it together, and there are still some beautiful things in their life . . .

You used to bake. Anything and everything. Rich cakes, full of fruit in brandy. Lovely light cakes that disappeared at the soft touch of a tongue. Fresh bread, dusty white or else brown and shining. You got up early every Saturday, and left the bedroom while the birds sang from the branches outside our window. Meanwhile, I yawned and moved into the small, warm place you left behind in the bed. A little later, when I woke, there would be a hot fog of smells. Sweet, heavy smells that filled our little flat. I would walk into the kitchen and find you standing there, hot coffee in your hand as you watched your cakes cooling down on the table.

That last time, you were baking because I had asked for something special. Something you hadn't tried before. A round cake – one my mother made for me when I was ten, to make me feel better because I was ill and had to stay at home all day. You and I were in bed, comfortable, reading our books. I had pulled at your side of the blanket and asked,

'Could you, would you make that cake for me?'

'How did she make it?' you wanted to know. 'What did it taste like?'

'Eggy. And not very sweet.'

You looked interested. 'Eggy?'

'Yes,' I said. 'And it was a very pale yellow in colour. And it was soft and light.'

'Eggy, soft and light. All right.' You smiled and moved your back close to mine.

The next morning, when I walked sleepily into the kitchen, I had forgotten about asking you for the cake. It was there, still warm, on the table. You cut a delicious, perfect slice and put it in my mouth.

That was almost a year ago. I remember now how sick you had become the day after. At first I thought it was because of the cake. Felt sure it was nothing more than a stomach cold. Silly of me. Remembering, I cannot stop myself laughing out loud. The sound comes out strange. One of our neighbours, a little old lady who always seems surprised to see me – I am too tall, too foreign-looking for this place – stops to smile. I return the smile, wondering at the difficulty of making the muscles round my mouth work.

I open the door of your favourite baker's shop. The first

time you took me there, you told me you had known the place since you were a child. I imagined you, five years old, reaching up to pick out a soft, sugared cake. Every week we used to stop there on the way to the market and look at the cakes in the window. One of them would catch your eye, and you'd spend the rest of the afternoon reading your richly coloured cookbooks, your fingers dancing over the words. There is, you always said, a cake for every occasion.

Now in our kitchen, instead of the eggs and butter and fruit, instead of the shining bowls and well-used bread boards, instead of all that, there are large tins piled high on the table, containing enriched milk and the powdered food which you hate so much, and a blender. The blender is a white, plastic, plain-looking machine. Ugly but necessary. I use it every morning and afternoon to make the thick, tasteless kind of soup which is the only food you can eat.

A bell rings as I enter the baker's. The only customer, an old Chinese man, is walking slowly up and down past all the cakes on show in their glass container. He stops, stares at me for a second, then walks back and starts looking carefully at the cakes again.

The lady owner, who has grey hair, looks up. Her hands, which she places in front of her, are small and covered with a fine dusting of white. I see that she recognizes me. 'How nice,' she had said, when I asked for the words Happy Lunar Eclipse to be written across the cake I was ordering.

'Hi, I'm here for my cake,' I say.

'Hello, yes, we have it ready.' She goes into the back of the shop to fetch it.

The old man is still trying to decide which of the cakes he wants. He bends over the glass container, then straightens up and smiles at me.

'I'm choosing something for my granddaughter,' he says, in clear, unhesitating English. 'Her mother's bringing her over to visit.'

I say nothing, only smile back in return.

'You have children?' he asks.

I learned a long time ago that the local people think nothing of asking personal questions. They ask them so warmly and with so much real interest that I answer right back. I surprised myself the first time that happened.

'No,' I say, thinking about the names you said you liked. Lara for a girl. Mark, if it's a boy.

'Oh. But you're married?' he asks, his grey head a little on one side.

'Yes. Just, not yet . . .' I give another smile, as best I can. He is about to say more when the lady returns with my cake in a box. It is a relief to stop talking to him, and I'm so pleased that I smile warmly at her. She puts the box down in front of me.

'Here it is,' she says, pushing it towards me and lifting the lid. 'OK?' she adds, smiling.

'Yes,' I say. 'Thank you. Goodbye.'

'Candles are inside the box,' she adds. 'Bye bye.'

I take the box from her carefully and turn to go. Behind me I hear the old man ask the lady for some help – he can't quite decide.

I check my watch as I walk home. Just past six. Over an

hour to go. The birds are calling out from the thick trees. I look up and watch a few clouds make their way quickly across the blue sky. As I stand there, red and brown fallen leaves, caught by the wind, collect around my shoes.

It takes me less than ten minutes to walk back, and soon I am unlocking the front door. I call out, like I do every time I come home. And, just like every single time, you call back. Your voice is quiet – it's hard to hear through the walls.

'Elise, I'm home!' I shout. When I'm around you, I'm cheerful, bright. Around you, I have to be. I drink a glass of water in the kitchen. Get myself together before I go in and see you. I know you've been ill now for months, but when I'm away for just a moment, an hour, I forget.

☾

The first time you went to hospital for chemotherapy, I watched the young nurse, shaky and unsure, push the needle in your arm, one, two, three times before she finally got it right. You had your eyes closed but your face was expressionless. You stayed like that all the way through. The machine kept going, slowly, achingly. Soon you started to shiver and said you were cold. I piled blankets on top of you, and still they weren't enough. You shook for two hours. At the end of it, you were exhausted. You fell asleep on the ride home in the car. I carried you in and put you to bed. I made sure you were asleep before I went to the second bathroom and bent over the toilet. I thought I was going to be sick. Then I sat on the cold floor until I heard you call out for me. Your voice sounded like a dream.

That same evening, your friends came over. Yan, whom

You fell asleep on the ride home in the car.
I carried you in and put you to bed.

you had grown up with, proudly offered you a rich, dark cake and sang, 'Happy first chemo, Elise!'

I watched you stop smiling for a moment. But then your eyes shone and you laughed and clapped along with the rest of them. I just stood and watched, hot with anger. You took a few bites, cautious little bites, before the sickness came. After an hour, everyone put their arms round you, said goodbye and left. I went with them to the door, and down to the street. As soon as we were a little way from the apartment, I took Yan by his collar and started shaking him. I think I shouted, 'Happy first chemo? Are you mad?'

Someone held me back then, but it took a few moments for me to realize what I was doing. When I stepped back, I saw that Yan's face was red and his mouth was thin. He put a hand on my shoulder and said, 'Will, it's all right. It's all right,' while looking everywhere else except at me.

Back inside, you were already asleep. I calmed myself down. I watched you as you breathed, your face shining in the moon's soft light.

(

I make myself busy now, putting everything away. The cake in the fridge, my wallet and keys on the dining table. The table is covered with well-worn books and papers about your disease – information that I've read and re-read many times. Then I walk the fifteen steps. That's how many it takes for me to get to you, from the moment I come through the front door.

You are very pale and painfully thin, lying in bed, half buried under the blanket. I enter the room, feeling my face go red. You look like a stranger. Has someone taken your place in the little time I've been away? You used to have rich, dark hair, but lying in our bed there is a girl with no hair at all on her head. She is watching me as I enter the room. Every time I go away and come back again, I feel I am entering someone else's flat. This is not our home. Not my place. Not our things, the countless silly little things that two people can collect in five years. Five years' worth of books, clothes, and stones from the beach. And photos taken with a blind hand, while our faces, full of light, are close to each other's. 'Where's Elise?' I think, while I stand in the doorway. But the minute I get near and you reach up to run your hand over my hair, reach up and pull me in with your small hands and look straight into me with your dark eyes, I see you again. You're right there. Hidden under that pale face. You're in there.

'Hey baby,' you say, 'how is it outside?'

'OK. There's a bit of wind, though. We're going to have to watch the eclipse through the window, OK? We don't want you to catch a cold.' I bend down and kiss you.

'Whatever you say.' You return to your book. I do my usual routine of tidying your blankets and making you comfortable, before you gently push my hands away.

'Take a rest,' you say. 'You've had a long day.'

I sigh and give in. I take one of the many books piled up by the bed and let myself lie down next to you. I open the book but simply stare at it, at one line on a page, letting it run in front of my eyes over and over again. Soon I hear you breathing deeply and look around to see you sleeping, with one finger marking the page where you stopped reading. I watch through the window as the sky lights up into bright orange and purple flames, while darkness slowly falls. Quietly I get out of bed and go into the kitchen for the cake and everything else that we need.

When I come back, you're already sitting up in bed.

'Is it time?' you ask.

'Soon,' I say, looking at my watch. 'Just ten minutes to go.'

I put the cake box in front of you. I lift up the lid and we both look inside.

There had been just enough room for the words. Eclipse had been written in the shape of a smile, just at the edge of the cake. You laugh, and tell me to put the candles in and light them. So I do. We wait a little while more. We look out of the window and watch as a dark shadow starts to cover the full moon and the silvery white becomes a yellowish-brown, until in the end all that's left in the half-light is a deep red ball giving out a dull, pinkish light in the night sky.

'Look,' you whisper, then blow out the candles.

I nod and reach for the knife, cutting a straight line down the middle of the cake. And then another. Then I pass it over. A delicious, perfect slice, onto your plate.

'Oh, red velvet cake,' you say. 'We've never had this before.'

The One-Armed Thief

KACHI A. OZUMBA

A story from Nigeria, retold by Clare West

Judges have a difficult job. They sit in a lawcourt and listen to stories – stories from the prosecutor, from the lawyers, from the accused. But whose story is the truth, and whose is a lie?

Abdul is confident that he understands the judge. But the judge is also confident that she understands Abdul . . .

For five years Abdul had been a beggar at the dusty Maraba crossroads. He had learnt how to work on people's feelings, like an actor. He always knew the right face to wear. There was one face which made people feel so sorry for him that his begging bowl rang with the sound of their coins. But there were some passers-by who kept their money tightly in their pockets and refused to give to beggars. For these people he had another face, one which made them feel so bad that they could not sleep at nights.

Today, in Abuja's main courtroom, as Abdul stood surrounded by police and lawyers, it was easy for him to decide which face to wear. 'This judge will never sleep well if she finds me guilty,' he thought to himself.

'Your worship, this man is a thief,' said the prosecutor,

pointing at Abdul. 'A shopkeeper caught him running away with a sack of rice.'

The judge's stare was almost frightening. Her sharp eyes shone with intelligence, and although she was only forty-something, she seemed to have several lifetimes of experience. Abdul met her look with dull, miserable eyes, then lowered his head and stared at his feet. It was an expression that had never failed him – the sad, thoughtful eyes of a dog, with the shyness of a trembling young bride.

'Your worship,' said Abdul's lawyer, 'this is the kind of stupid mistake the Nigerian police are famous for. How can a one-armed man steal a fifty-kilogram sack of rice? Even I cannot lift that sack onto my back with my two arms. I understand that the accused had a regular begging place outside the shop. He informs me, and I truly believe him, that the shopkeeper threatened to do anything possible to move him away from the front of the shop. He has been falsely accused!'

The judge's eyes showed that a battle between feeling and reason was taking place inside her head. Abdul lifted the stump of his right arm and scratched his face with it. His arm had been cut off at the elbow, and the stump was clearly visible. It looked so ugly that most people felt very sorry for him as soon as they saw it.

'This is not the first time this man has stolen—' the prosecutor said.

Abdul's lawyer jumped up. 'Your worship, the prosecutor is being unfair. It's true that the accused was once a thief. In fact, a court in another part of the country ordered his right

Abdul stared down at the sack of rice, which was on the floor between the rows of lawyers, and a sigh escaped his lips.

arm to be cut off as a punishment. But that was years ago, and since then he has stolen nothing.'

'We know that he has been involved in seven recent robberies,' the prosecutor continued. 'Your worship, believe me, hardened thieves like him don't change easily.'

The cool wind blowing into the courtroom failed to dry Abdul's hot, wet forehead. He shook his head slowly. He stared down at the sack of rice, which was on the floor between the rows of lawyers, and a sigh escaped his lips. It was the long-suffering sigh of a man who accepts that he is going to be punished for something he did not do.

The judge's eyes were fierce as she spoke to the prosecutor. 'You bad man! You're supposed to prosecute people who have done wrong, not attack those who are innocent! Have you no heart left in you?'

Her expression softened as she turned to Abdul. 'The court apologizes to you. You can go home. And take the sack of rice with you. I hope it will help you to forget all this unpleasantness. Go on, carry the sack of rice and go home right now!'

Abdul could not believe his ears. He turned around, and in two steps he had reached the sack of rice. He put his left arm around it, dropped on one knee, touched his head to the ground, and with a sudden, fast movement of his back and arm, lifted the sack onto his shoulders.

He stood up again with difficulty, bent over by the heavy sack. 'Thank you very much, your worship,' he said, trying to catch his breath.

'Thank you too,' the judge said. 'Police, arrest him!'

GLOSSARY

afterbirth   the material that comes out of a female body after a
   baby has been born, and which fed and protected the baby
altar   a table in a holy place, (*here*) in a private house
baseball cap   a cap with a long peak in front
belly   the part of the body below the chest
bull   an adult male cow
calf (*plural* **calves**)   a young cow
candle   a round stick of wax which burns to give light
casino   a building where people play gambling games for money
chemotherapy (*informal* **chemo**)   treating a disease (e.g. cancer)
   with chemicals
closet (*NAmE*)   a cupboard, (*BrE*) a place for storing things
coffin   a long box in which a dead person is placed
court   the place where judges and lawyers listen to law cases
courtyard   an open space surrounded by the walls of a building
cub (*here*)   a young polar bear
docks   the place in a port where ships are loaded and unloaded
fan (*n*)   a thing held in the hand and waved, to make the air cooler
foot (*plural* **feet** or **foot**)   a unit of length (= 30.48 centimetres)
frame (*n*)   a structure of wood to hold a picture in position
funeral   the ceremony of burying a dead person
fur   the hair on the skin of an animal
garbage bin   a large container with a lid, used for rubbish
grasshopper   an insect with long back legs, which jumps
growl (*v*)   to make a low, threatening sound in the throat
**hindquarters, forequarters, sausages, mince, top-side steak, fillet
   steak**   different cuts and types of meat at a butcher's
hunt (*v*)   to chase and kill wild animals
illegal immigration   when people enter a country without
   permission and try to stay there permanently

Jerry Seinfeld an American actor, known for playing himself in
the long-running TV show *Seinfeld* (1989–1998)
joss sticks thin wooden sticks that burn slowly and smell sweet
Jungle Energy Bar a healthy snack food
licensed butcher a person who cuts up and sells meat in a shop
lizard a small animal with four short legs and a long tail
lunar eclipse when the earth passes between the moon and the
sun, and for a while hides the moon
make-up creams, etc. used to make a face look more attractive
mattress the soft part of a bed that you lie on
mealie-meal a coarse flour made from maize
mourning showing sadness because someone has died
nod (*v*) to move your head up and down in agreement
palm tree a tropical tree with a lot of long leaves at the top
Pink Floyd a successful English rock band, popular in the late
1960s, known for the unusual sounds they produced
pirate a person on a ship who attacks and steals from other ships
polar bear a wild animal with thick white fur and sharp claws,
which lives near the North Pole
policy paying money to an insurance company, which promises
to pay you if you have an accident, become ill, etc.
pray to speak privately to God
priest a person who performs religious ceremonies
prosecutor a lawyer who speaks against the accused person in
court
red velvet cake a cake with a dark red or reddish-brown colour
relief a feeling of gladness that a problem has gone away
rickshaw a kind of bicycle 'taxi', used in some Asian countries
sack (*n*) a large bag with no handles, made of strong material
sacred basil a plant with sweet-smelling leaves used in cooking,
which is considered holy (sacred) in India
sari a kind of dress worn by women in South Asia

scent (*n*)   the particular smell that something has
shanty town   an area where poor people live in shanties (small houses built of bits and pieces of wood, metal, cardboard, etc.)
shiver   to shake slightly because you are cold, frightened, etc.
shorts   short trousers that end above or at the knee
show (*n*)   a programme on television or the radio
sigh (*v*)   to let out a long deep breath to show you are sad, etc.
slippers   a pair of loose soft shoes that you wear in the house
squat   to sit on your heels with your knees close to your body
stump   the short part of an arm, after the rest has been cut off
superstition   the belief that some events bring good or bad luck
surfing   riding waves while standing on a narrow board
sweep   to clean a floor using a brush on a long handle
swollen   grown bigger than usual
thrift store (*NAmE*)   a shop that sells clothes and other things given by people to raise money for poor people
tobacco   the dried leaves of a plant, used for making cigarettes
vagrant   a person who has no home or job
wetsuit (*informal* **wettie**)   a piece of clothing made of rubber that fits the whole body closely and keeps you warm in the sea
windscreen wiper   a blade with a rubber edge that moves across a car's windows to clear rain away
yard (*NAmE*)   a garden or a piece of land next to a house
your worship   a polite way of speaking to a judge

ACTIVITIES

Before Reading

Before you read each story, read the introduction on the first page. Then use the questions below to help you make some guesses about the stories.

1   *A Place to Stay* (story introduction page 1). What do you think happens to Lakshmi and Ramu? They . . .
    a) become homeless. b) rent a room. c) buy an apartment.

2   *The Silk Fan* (story introduction page 6). What kind of secret do you think there is in Lin Lin's family, and what could be the message she has for her aunt?

3   *Meeting Susamatekkie* (story introduction page 16). Will the man from the city and the young Basutho man get on well together, do you think? What might the problems be?

4   *Clean Sheets* (story introduction page 21). What do you think a 'clean sheet' means?
    a) a healthy lifestyle   b) a house free of dirt   c) a fresh start

5   *Or Be Killed* (story introduction page 25). Can you predict what situation Cam is going to find herself in, and how she will react to it?

6   *Down South* (story introduction page 30). What are the dangers of surfing as a sport? Can you guess what is going to happen to Mike and Ben?

7 *An Old Wife's Tale* (story introduction page 35). Which
   statement do you agree with? An old wife's tale is . . .
   a) a superstition, which is usually untrue.
   b) a kind of proverb, which is always true.

8 *Swamiji's Ring* (story introduction page 39). Who do you
   think will go to a fortune-teller in this story, Rahul or his
   mother? Do you think magic can make a difference to their
   lives?

9 *The Policy* (story introduction page 45). What do you think
   Arnold Snell is planning to do?
   a) kill his wife   b) leave his wife   c) kill himself

10 *Anywhere But Here* (story introduction page 50). What
    reasons would anyone have for travelling inside a container
    on a ship? What practical problems would there be?

11 *Recycling* (story introduction page 55). Which statement
    do you agree with? Recycling is a way of . . .
    a) getting rid of rubbish by burning it or burying it.
    b) re-using things which people no longer want.

12 *Eclipse* (story introduction page 59). Is this going to be a
    sad story, do you think? Are Will and Elise still going to be
    in love by the end of the story? What will the sadness be?

13 *The One-Armed Thief* (story introduction page 68). Who is
    the accused, and what do you think he is accused of?

ACTIVITIES

After Reading

1 **Several of these stories have open endings. What do you think happens next in each story? Add your own ideas, if you like, and then write a short paragraph for your chosen ending.**

The Silk Fan

1 Lin Lin leaves the house and never sees her family again.

2 Lin Lin is ill for a long time, but Ah Kim looks after her.

Or Be Killed

1 The bear walks away and Cam is safe.

2 A hunter comes along and shoots the bear.

3 Cam is killed by the bear.

Down South

1 Mike and Ben drown in the ocean.

2 Mike and Ben have the best surfing day of their lives.

An Old Wife's Tale

1 The husband returns home.

2 A friend brings the husband's body home.

Swamiji's Ring

1 Rahul's mother doesn't speak to him for a week.

2 Rahul says he is sorry and promises to visit Swamiji with his mother.

Recycling

1 Judith gives the leather suitcase to the next vagrant who comes.

2 Judith puts her clothes into the leather suitcase and goes away to start a new life.

2 **Here are the thoughts of thirteen characters (one from each story). Who is thinking, which stories are they from, and what has just happened?**

1 'I'll put some oil in the pan, take a handful of rice . . . Silly boy, he thinks he knows everything! But he's a good son, deep down – he hates to see me cry. In a minute he'll be in, to say I could be right . . .'

2 'Let's see what she's put in her bin today. Ah! It's a gold wedding ring. That'll be worth a lot. Thanks, lady! So she's putting her marriage in the bin. That's sad. Time to move on, lady, time to move on . . . I'll leave her this . . .'

3 'Too tired. Too hot. Desperate for tea. I'll just sit here for a minute and let her do the talking. I know it'll be a small room, but there's nowhere else. Will it be expensive? There's no way we can work any harder!'

4 'Stupid girl, always asking about her father! And now attacking me in front of my dead husband and the whole family – it's too much. It's time to tell her about my big strong husband and his pretty little sister . . .'

5 'I know it's terrible for him, seeing her get worse day by day, but it's terrible for us too. And there was no need for him to attack me like that, and shout at me like a madman. I don't think I'll visit her again – it's too painful.'

6 'He's a good actor, this one, and he's made everyone here feel sorry for him. But why was she so angry with me – I'm just doing my job! And I think he's going to get away with it. Oh no, look what he's just done! Oh, clever judge!'

7 'This white man with yellow teeth is a strange man! He has a house in the town, but he likes sleeping in a tent, on these cold nights! But he has promised me a ride in a motor car if I visit him . . .'

8 'Oh, that's better, I felt so restless in the house. The air's really fresh and cold out here – I can breathe properly . . . Hey, what's that large white shape ahead? Oh my God!'

9 'I'm really not sure about this. My wettie's wet, my feet are like ice. Those waves are just so big! I don't like it. There he goes, straight in. It's me next. One, two, three . . .'

10 'Close the door – that's it – and walk away. So easy. Walk away to a new life. I'll never have to see him again, cook his meals, wash his clothes, clean up after him. How will he manage on his own? Well, that's not my problem now!'

11 'They're lucky to have me – they'd die of hunger without me! I took all the risks getting those first tins of food, but they didn't even say thank you! Next time I'll do it differently, and they won't even know . . .'

12 'There's good luck and bad luck on every trip. I've caught a lot of big fish this time, that's true, but I've hurt my arm really badly. Maybe the old woman is right – I shouldn't come so far out . . .'

13 'Oh! Oh! Oh! Get a glass of water! A chair! A doctor! An ambulance! No, not for him, stupid, for me! Oh, the sight of so much blood's too much for me, I've never been strong! Hold me, I'm going to fall!'

3 **Discuss your answers to these questions about the stories.**

   1 If you could help one person from one of these stories,
      who would it be, and how would you help them?

   2 Are there any characters who need some good advice?
      Which characters are they, and in which stories? What
      advice would you give them?

   3 Many characters do wrong or foolish things. Who, in your
      opinion, does the worst thing? Give your reasons.

4 **Here is a short poem (a kind of poem called a haiku) about
   one of the stories. Which of the thirteen stories is it about?**

   No sign of the man.
   His anxious wife falls asleep.
   Dawn brings little hope.

   Here is another haiku.
   Which story is this
   one about?

   Planning for this day
   The angry years pass slowly
   Great will be her shame!

   **A haiku is a Japanese poem, which is always in three lines, and
   the three lines always have 5, 7, and 5 syllables each, like this:**

   | No | sign | of | the | man | = 5 syllables
   | His | anx | ious | wife | falls | a | sleep | = 7 syllables
   | Dawn | brings | lit | tle | hope | = 5 syllables

   **Now write your own haiku, one for each of the other eleven
   stories. Think about what each story is really about. What are
   the important ideas for you? Remember to keep to three lines
   of 5, 7, 5 syllables each.**

ABOUT THE AUTHORS

SWAPNA KISHORE

Swapna Kishore lives in Bangalore, India, with her family. She is a writer and also a volunteer who helps families looking after elders suffering from dementia. Swapna has written technical books, training material, and fiction. Her story, *A Place to Stay*, was one of the winners in the 2005 Commonwealth Short Story Competition. She says: 'I write about personal things that touch me, and things that make me wonder. And when I am puzzled, I write to understand things.'

TEOH CHOON EAN

Teoh Choon Ean is Malaysian. She has been a teacher, an educational project manager, and a teacher trainer. She wrote her prize-winning novel, *Nine Lives*, she says, in just six days, typing almost non-stop. 'I decided to sit down with a one-liner idea and write from the heart.' She wrote *The Silk Fan* after reading about the meaning of 'Autumn Fan' in a book of Chinese symbols. It was at the time of her father's funeral, and she wanted to record the local funeral traditions for people to read about in future.

TOD COLLINS

Tod Collins' family came to Natal in South Africa in the 1850s. He studied veterinary science and now works as a vet in a small country town. He climbs mountains in his spare time, and enjoys writing stories about his adventures as a vet and his experiences in the mountains of KwaZulu-Natal and Lesotho. *Meeting Susamatekkie* won a prize in the 2007 True Stories of KwaZulu-Natal Competition. Tod has also published a collection of his stories, titled *'Til the Cows Come Home*.

SUE SEAH

Sue Seah is an award-winning architect and writer from Singapore. She was one of the winners of the 2006 Commonwealth Short Story Competition. Her story *Clean Sheets* was written while she was living in Toronto, Canada. She currently resides in Chicago with her husband and daughter, where she continues to pursue her writing.

ELISE MOSER

Elise Moser was born in Brooklyn, New York, and grew up in the USA, but has lived in Montreal, Canada, all her adult life. She has worked in a bookstore and sold books across Canada. Her short stories have been published or broadcast in several countries, and her novel *Because I Have Loved and Hidden It* came out in 2009. She is vegetarian, and tries to live simply. She wrote *Or Be Killed* because she believes that humans should reconsider how we share the planet with others.

PETER JAMES

Peter James lives in Melbourne, Australia, with his wife and two daughters. A keen surfer for thirty years, he has recently started making his own surfboards. When he is not working in his shed, or out surfing, or repairing Citroen 2CV cars, he writes advertising copy. Peter says that his story *Down South* 'captures the essence of what it's like to surf off the harsh, remote south-western coastline of Victoria in the middle of winter.'

LUKE JORSLING

Luke Jorsling was born in Trinidad, West Indies. He used to write plays, and two of his playscripts won national competitions, in 1998 and 2001. Now, however, he focuses on writing poetry and short prose. *An Old Wife's Tale* was partly inspired by his parents' practice of putting an empty glass down over the occasional grasshopper that flew into their home at night; this was supposed to bring riches to the family.

RIDJAL NOOR

Ridjal Noor was born in Singapore, to Indian parents who had migrated there. He has a degree in Communications and Media Management, and runs a small design firm in Singapore. He started writing when he was seventeen, and in his stories he explores the Indian way of life, researching his forefathers' history and culture. His writing has been published in Malaysia, Australia, and the United Kingdom.

SYLVIA McNICKLE

Sylvia McNickle is a registered nurse and has been a part-time writer for many years, before moving to a wild part of Australia in order to focus on writing and music. She writes plays for the local theatre group, and plays and sings in a three-piece band. She lives on a family community acreage in a small stone cottage on the edge of a large tree-fringed pond. She says, 'I am interested in the traps people get themselves into,' and thinks perhaps that is why she wrote *The Policy*.

C. J. ONYIA

Chidi Jasmine Onyia was born in Leeds, England, and moved to Nigeria in the late 1970s. Later she returned to the UK, and studied International Development at the University of Liverpool. She has three children and lives with her family in Cheshire, UK. She says that these days a lot of young Nigerians want to leave their country in search of a better life, but it is a dangerous thing to do, and some of them lose their lives every year. That is the story she tells in *Anywhere But Here*.

ELEANOR VERBICKY-TODD

Eleanor Verbicky-Todd grew up in Edmonton, Canada. She has a degree in English Literature from the University of Alberta, and also studied at the University of Oklahoma. Her stories have been broadcast and published, and her short fiction has won prizes in several competitions. *Recycling* was one of the winners in the 2006 Commonwealth Short Story Competition. Her interests include history, travelling, and walking in the Rocky Mountains, near her home in Canada.

LEE JING-JING

Lee Jing-Jing was born in Singapore and lived there until her early twenties, when she was accepted on the Oxford University MA in Creative Writing course. Since then she has published both poetry and short stories in literary journals, written a short novel set in Singapore, and started work on a longer novel. She wrote the story, *Eclipse*, while she was on a three-hour bus ride in the UK, from Stansted Airport to Oxford.

KACHI A. OZUMBA

Kachi A. Ozumba is a Nigerian-born novelist and short-story writer, who lives in Newcastle, UK. His story, *What's in a Name*, won the Arts Council England's Decibel Penguin Prize in 2006. His first novel, *The Shadow of a Smile* (2009), was shortlisted for two awards, and *The One-Armed Thief* was a winner in the 2009 Commonwealth Short Story Competition (Africa region). Kachi has been writer-in-residence at the Beverley Literature Festival, and a judge in two literary competitions.

OXFORD BOOKWORMS LIBRARY

Classics • Crime & Mystery • Factfiles • Fantasy & Horror
Human Interest • Playscripts • Thriller & Adventure
True Stories • World Stories

The OXFORD BOOKWORMS LIBRARY provides enjoyable reading in English, with a wide range of classic and modern fiction, non-fiction, and plays. It includes original and adapted texts in seven carefully graded language stages, which take learners from beginner to advanced level. An overview is given on the next pages.

All Stage 1 titles are available as audio recordings, as well as over eighty other titles from Starter to Stage 6. All Starters and many titles at Stages 1 to 4 are specially recommended for younger learners. Every Bookworm is illustrated, and Starters and Factfiles have full-colour illustrations.

The OXFORD BOOKWORMS LIBRARY also offers extensive support. Each book contains an introduction to the story, notes about the author, a glossary, and activities. Additional resources include tests and worksheets, and answers for these and for the activities in the books. There is advice on running a class library, using audio recordings, and the many ways of using Oxford Bookworms in reading programmes. Resource materials are available on the website <www.oup.com/bookworms>.

The *Oxford Bookworms Collection* is a series for advanced learners. It consists of volumes of short stories by well-known authors, both classic and modern. Texts are not abridged or adapted in any way, but carefully selected to be accessible to the advanced student.

You can find details and a full list of titles in the *Oxford Bookworms Library Catalogue* and *Oxford English Language Teaching Catalogues*, and on the website <www.oup.com/bookworms>.

THE OXFORD BOOKWORMS LIBRARY
GRADING AND SAMPLE EXTRACTS

STARTER • 250 HEADWORDS

present simple – present continuous – imperative –
can/cannot, must – *going to* (future) – simple gerunds …

Her phone is ringing – but where is it?

Sally gets out of bed and looks in her bag. No phone. She looks under the bed. No phone. Then she looks behind the door. There is her phone. Sally picks up her phone and answers it. *Sally's Phone*

STAGE 1 • 400 HEADWORDS

… past simple – coordination with *and, but, or* –
subordination with *before, after, when, because, so* …

I knew him in Persia. He was a famous builder and I worked with him there. For a time I was his friend, but not for long. When he came to Paris, I came after him – I wanted to watch him. He was a very clever, very dangerous man. *The Phantom of the Opera*

STAGE 2 • 700 HEADWORDS

… present perfect – *will* (future) – (*don't*) *have to, must not, could* –
comparison of adjectives – simple *if* clauses – past continuous –
tag questions – *ask/tell* + infinitive …

While I was writing these words in my diary, I decided what to do. I must try to escape. I shall try to get down the wall outside. The window is high above the ground, but I have to try. I shall take some of the gold with me – if I escape, perhaps it will be helpful later. *Dracula*

STAGE 3 • 1000 HEADWORDS

... should, may – present perfect continuous – *used to* – past perfect –
causative – relative clauses – indirect statements ...

Of course, it was most important that no one should see Colin, Mary, or Dickon entering the secret garden. So Colin gave orders to the gardeners that they must all keep away from that part of the garden in future. *The Secret Garden*

STAGE 4 • 1400 HEADWORDS

... past perfect continuous – passive (simple forms) –
would conditional clauses – indirect questions –
relatives with *where/when* – gerunds after prepositions/phrases ...

I was glad. Now Hyde could not show his face to the world again. If he did, every honest man in London would be proud to report him to the police. *Dr Jekyll and Mr Hyde*

STAGE 5 • 1800 HEADWORDS

... future continuous – future perfect –
passive (modals, continuous forms) –
would have conditional clauses – modals + perfect infinitive ...

If he had spoken Estella's name, I would have hit him. I was so angry with him, and so depressed about my future, that I could not eat the breakfast. Instead I went straight to the old house. *Great Expectations*

STAGE 6 • 2500 HEADWORDS

... passive (infinitives, gerunds) – advanced modal meanings –
clauses of concession, condition

When I stepped up to the piano, I was confident. It was as if I knew that the prodigy side of me really did exist. And when I started to play, I was so caught up in how lovely I looked that I didn't worry how I would sound. *The Joy Luck Club*

MORE WORLD STORIES FROM BOOKWORMS

The Meaning of Gifts: Stories from Turkey
STAGE 1   RETOLD BY JENNIFER BASSETT

Cries from the Heart: Stories from Around the World*
STAGE 2   RETOLD BY JENNIFER BASSETT

Changing their Skies: Stories from Africa
STAGE 2   RETOLD BY JENNIFER BASSETT

Songs from the Soul: Stories from Around the World
STAGE 2   RETOLD BY JENNIFER BASSETT

The Long White Cloud: Stories from New Zealand
STAGE 3   RETOLD BY CHRISTINE LINDOP

Dancing with Strangers: Stories from Africa*
STAGE 3   RETOLD BY CLARE WEST

Playing with Fire: Stories from the Pacific Rim*
STAGE 3   RETOLD BY JENNIFER BASSETT

Leaving No Footprint: Stories from Asia *
STAGE 3   RETOLD BY CLARE WEST

A Cup of Kindness: Stories from Scotland
STAGE 3   RETOLD BY JENNIFER BASSETT

Doors to a Wider Place: Stories from Australia
STAGE 4   RETOLD BY CHRISTINE LINDOP

Land of my Childhood: Stories from South Asia**
STAGE 4   RETOLD BY CLARE WEST

The Price of Peace: Stories from Africa
STAGE 4   RETOLD BY CHRISTINE LINDOP

A Time of Waiting: Stories from Around the World
STAGE 4   RETOLD BY CLARE WEST

Treading on Dreams: Stories from Ireland
STAGE 5   RETOLD BY CLARE WEST

Gazing at Stars: Stories from Asia
STAGE 6   RETOLD BY CLARE WEST

** Winner: Language Learner Literature Awards
* Finalist: Language Learner Literature Awards